PISCES

PISCES

Let your Sun sign show you the way
to a happy and fulfilling life

Marion Williamson & Pam Carruthers

SIRIUS

This edition published in 2021 by Sirius Publishing, a
division of
Arcturus Publishing Limited,
26/27 Bickels Yard, 151–153 Bermondsey Street,
London SE1 3HA

ISBN: 978-1-3988-0862-1
AD008772UK

Printed in China

CONTENTS

Introduction

*W*elcome, Pisces! You have just taken a step towards what might become a lifelong passion. When astrology gets under your skin, there's no going back. Astrology helps you understand yourself and the people around you, and its dazzling insights become more fascinating the deeper you go.

Just as the first humans turned to the life-giving Sun for sustenance and guidance, your astrological journey begins with your Sun sign of Pisces. First, we delve deeply into the heart of what makes you tick, then we'll continue to unlock your cosmic potential by exploring love, your career and health, where you might prefer to live, and how you get along with family and friends.

Then it's over to gifted astrologer, Pam Carruthers, for her phenomenal birthdate analysis, where she reveals personality insights for every single specific Piscean birthday.

In the last part of the book we get right inside how astrology works by revealing the different layers that will help you understand your own birth chart and offer the planetary tools to get you started.

Are you ready, Pisces? Let's take your glorious imagination for a swim …

CUSP DATES FOR PISCES
19 February – 20 March

The exact time of the Sun's entry into each zodiac sign varies every year, so it's impossible to list them all. If you were born a day either side of the dates above, you're a 'cusp' baby. This means you may feel like you're a blend of Pisces/Aquarius or Pisces/Aries or you may instinctively just know that you're one sign right to your core.

Going deeper

If you want to know once and for all whether you're an Aquarius, Pisces or Aries, you can look up your birthdate in a planetary ephemeris, of which there are plenty online. (See page 102 for more information.) This shows the exact moment the Sun moved into a new zodiac sign for the month you were born.

The Pisces personality

*Y*ou are Pisces, the Fish, the most compassionate and spiritual of all the zodiac signs, and your empathy is almost telepathic. Your zodiac symbol is depicted as two fish swimming in opposite directions, representing your constant flipping between fantasy and reality, and your immensely sensitive nature and boundless imagination means it's sometimes challenging for you to feel rooted in the here and now. You're a deeply intuitive and emotional Water sign, reflecting the fathomless, mysterious power of the ocean, and sometimes you feel swept away on waves of feeling. You are ruled by elusive, ethereal Neptune, the planet of magic and illusion, and you have a reputation for being the most wonderfully creative person, even if you sometimes view the world through rose-tinted spectacles.

Each sign of the zodiac is thought to embody a little of the wisdom and lessons of the signs preceding it. As Pisces is the last of the 12 signs, you have absorbed all the wisdom, joy, pain and fears of the other zodiac characters. This explains why you have a rather blurred, obscure sense of self, and why you are more tuned to the collective psyche than anyone else. You're not entirely sure you want to be here – and as you contain the seeds of wisdom from all the other signs – on some level you feel like you may have already been here, seen, and done it all already. Earthly reality can be beastly and, as a spiritually inclined Fish, you long to return to the ocean of universal consciousness.

KEEPING IT REAL

The fact is, Pisces, you are here on earth (for now anyway) and you must connect to the life around you. It's your job to find beauty and meaning in the real, bricks-and-mortar, warts and all, everyday world. For you to feel truly alive and happy, your lesson is to step outside your limitless imagination and learn to be a person in your own right. As someone who understands the suffering of life on earth more intensely than most, you can form the deepest connections with the people who need your faith, kindness and compassion.

You're in a unique position to give people who have lost their way something wonderful to believe in, whether that's a spiritual or religious belief, faith in human kindness or hope and delight at the breathtaking beauty in the world.

You may not even be aware that you're tuned into a different wavelength to everyone else. You can be talking to a friend, and a fleeting thought or image will suddenly pop into your mind. Sometimes you feel like you've been whacked on the head with a newspaper with a giant headline about what's going on with your pal, and at other times it will be a more subtle experience. But you'll still know without doubt that what you've experienced is real. It might be something they're hiding, or at times you can just tell what's going to happen to him or her. It may be hard to convince your more down-to-earth friends that you notice things about them that they don't appear to acknowledge themselves, but you also have plenty of supporters that know from experience what an eerie ability you have. But then this is just one of your many skills.

EXQUISITELY CREATIVE

The flipside to being aware of life's joys as well as disappointments is that you know real beauty when you find it. A pretty weed growing through a crack in the pavement can fill your heart with joy, and a smile from a stranger in a supermarket instantly restores your faith in humanity. Your intense sensitivity allows creativity to stream through you, and you're never happier than when in full flow. You have too little ego, and value your privacy too much to thrust your ideas and creations on the outside world, and you usually underestimate your capabilities. But creatively you're capable of creating the most moving pieces of music, evocative poetry, and exquisite works of art.

ESCAPIST DREAMWORLDS

Much of your inspiration comes from your dreams

or seems funnelled from a different plane of existence altogether. Your dream recall is usually incredibly detailed, often in full technicolour with dramatic scripts and rolling credits before you wake up. Some Pisces remember the faces of people from their dreams so clearly, that they would recognise them in the street. You're connected with levels of consciousness that the rest of us are not yet conscious of, and some Pisces can attain different states of awareness by meditating, through different sleep states or by just daydreaming. Sometimes you'll go anywhere just to get away from real life!

On some level you can't quite believe you have incarnated into this clunky, ugly world where everyone feels lonely. When you're tuned into other planes of existence, earthly life can feel heavy. Your desire for escapism is probably the most difficult for you to master because why go through the effort and disappointment of finding a job, looking for someone to love, and taking care of yourself, when you can get lost in books, sex or daydreaming? And, of course, there's alternative realities to visit where you can blot out the real world completely.

Through identifying and empathising with the challenging or dramatic experiences of the people around you, you will eventually realise that the reason you're here – and the lesson you need to complete your karma – is to help the lost and lonely souls in the world. And you can't do that if your own soul is flapping about listlessly looking for meaning!

LIFE'S CURRENCY

To make a dent in the physical world you're going to have to get your head around money, which you'll either see as the root of all evil, or as an elusive resource that pours through you like water through a sieve. You can't say no to people in trouble just as you can't ignore those heart-breaking television campaigns for animal charities or for people who desperately need help. You'll see one sad looking doggy and give your last ten pounds to an animal shelter before realising you need it for your rent, bus fare to work – or your dinner!

It can take you quite a long time to figure out that money doesn't arrive or vanish on a whim. You have faith that money will materialise when you need it mostly because that's exactly what it seems to have done in the past. But it's a pretty unreliable way to get along in life, and at some point you'll want some stability – a job, an address of your own, and perhaps a family, pets or houseplants to look after.

When you see what a difference your own money can make to help or care for other people, you'll feel more motivated to bring it in consistently. You are best suited to work where you are able to relieve others' pain or disillusionment, maybe in a job campaigning for a homeless charity, as a doctor or nurse, a psychotherapist or as an alternative health practitioner. Your commitment to any deserving cause will shine through you and impress any employer with your dedication.

You'll also attract money by exchanging it for the wonderful manifestations of your rich imagination. But as you're inclined to underestimate your talents, you might need a little encouragement to get started. If you haven't already, you could begin by building an online audience for your astonishing art, fine dressmaking skills, or marvellously inventive fiction.

YOU'RE WORTH IT

Not everyone is as open and understanding as you. You're a wonderful listener, and your empathic nature encourages others to share their secrets, worries and woes. And as you have an impressionable, boundary-less Neptune as your ruling planet, it's hard for you to separate your own thoughts and feelings from those of others. This is why it's important that you get enough time on your own to recover your sense of self. You have unparalleled skills for bringing beauty and happiness to others through your selfless deeds – and just being yourself. But before you give yourself away, you must work on what it is that you love doing and what makes you happy. If you're going to inspire, uplift and encourage people who are confused about where they're going – you can't also be lost!

VIRGO LESSON

We share many attributes with our opposite zodiac sign, and these polarising characters can also show something we may be missing – or need to concentrate on in our own personalities. Like you, Virgo is modest, gentle and wants to help make life a better place for others. And while most Pisces haven't yet accepted that they have actually incarnated into a body, on Earth, Virgo teaches you the practical skills you need to master to enjoy being here. Something of an expert at looking after the essential details: finding work, looking after health, being on time and getting organised, Virgo teaches you to deal with what is in front of right now. Once you are responsible for your own well-being, you'll be a happier person and the rest should fall into place. You'll feel less distracted by your own woes and will have more energy and confidence to take care of the rest of humanity!

Pisces
Motto

WHEN I WAS
TOLD I WAS BEING
UNREALISTIC,
I ALMOST FELL OFF
MY UNICORN.

Pisces in love

*P*isces is depicted as two fish swimming in opposite directions, simultaneously experiencing conscious and unconscious, heaven and hell, and nowhere do these extremes feel more apparent than in your love life. As far as you're concerned, the perfect union of romantic love is the closest to heaven you can be. You know that the merging of twin souls could make you feel whole again, perhaps because you've already had a taste of it in this life – or been there in a past one. Unconsciously or not, you wish for romantic love to save you, to swallow you whole and tell you that nothing else matters.

POETIC MERMAID SOUL

You are eternally hopeful that you'll meet the perfect person who makes all the pain go away and gives you meaning to your life. But sometimes in your love dreams you project what you so badly want onto another person, and you'll make-believe it's true. You may have already thought you were in love a few times only to have stark reality pull you aside for a few harsh words.

You want to believe the lovely things you hear other people say are true, and learning that people are 'just being nice' to avoid hurting your feelings is a bitter pill to swallow. You hurt like nobody else, but because you allow yourself to feel so much emotion, you are rather brilliant at processing your feelings and moving on.

You're quite hypnotised by the lure of losing yourself in another, and the possibility of romance is so enticing that you can swim from one affair to the other, in search of the person who completely sweeps you away. And sometimes you do meet someone who fits the bill … for a while. But when they eventually reveal themselves to be real people with morning breath and terrible taste in music, you feel a little cheated.

FISHY FAIRY TALE

You're so in love with love that you can't help but hope the next person you feel attracted to will prove all the fairy tales right. But that's a tall order for anyone to live up to. Your intended may even feel that you're looking right through them to some mystical reflection that bears little resemblance to her or him. If you're being realistic you might even feel, in some of your less limerent moments, that perhaps your reverence has very little to do with the flesh and blood person who just cooked you scrambled eggs or bought you tickets to see your favourite film.

HONESTLY, PISCES

When you care for others as deeply as you do it's essential that you try to see things clearly, and that's not that easy with ambiguous, hazy Neptune as your ruling planet. When you want something to be true, you'll often take the line of least resistance by pulling the wool over your own eyes rather than dealing with what's really there. You find confrontation hugely uncomfortable and will avoid asking loved ones direct questions for fear of finding out the truth. But that's exactly what you need to keep yourself rooted in the real world.

Honesty is what you need most from your relationships because when you become more skilled at dealing with your own reality, you'll be a much better judge of other people's character and intentions – which should cut a heap of heartbreak from your life.

TRICKY EMOTIONS

You have an amazing ability to find beauty and magic in sadness and tragedy – and you can be strangely attracted to people who face real difficulties. But you'll need to have your reality head screwed on if you feel the line between compassion and romantic love beginning to get fuzzy. Go in with your eyes fully open and enlist some practical Earth sign friends to keep your heart from slipping into fantasy mode.

Most compatible
love signs

Scorpio – you're one of the few people that can see past Scorpio's deadpan expression to the deep well of emotion inside – and you like it!

Virgo – your opposite sign of Virgo gently and kindly shows you how to live in the real world without making it seem too unpleasant.

Cancer – you're on the same level emotionally, both sensitive and careful with each other's hearts.

Least compatible
love signs

Aries – there's no sugar coating with Aries; they're as blunt and on-the-nose as they come. You need a bit more fairy tale and stardust than that!

Gemini – Gemini usually floats on the surface of things when you like to dive in as deeply as possible.

Leo – you need time away from people to feel like an individual, and Leo feeds off attention to feel like they're valid.

Pisces at work

*Y*ou absorb the atmosphere of the pond you swim in, so your working environment is particularly important to you. In your younger years you may spend a few years swimming from place to place, discovering what appeals and your preferred way of working. You'll probably have discovered that you prefer working quietly in the background. But anyone who thinks that because you keep yourself to yourself that you're not doing anything of note is usually deceived. When it's your time to talk about what you've been working on, or your employer asks for results, you'll modestly render everyone speechless with your imaginative, well thought-out piece of creative genius.

TRUTHFUL TACTICS

If you've been in the same job for too long, you may feel the waters stagnate, but as you dislike confrontation, you can become complacent and settle for the line of least resistance. Although it scares you silly sometimes, the truth is actually your greatest friend. Pluck up the courage to have a candid conversation with your employer if you feel things are going nowhere. You may be surprised to find that your talents will be missed, and that your job can be adapted or changed, reviving you with a refreshing new tank of water to swim in. Magical things happen when you turn to the truth, even when it feels so outside your comfort zone that it might break you in two.

FISHY CAREERS

You're the artist of the zodiac, able to communicate what cannot be otherwise expressed, through paint, music, pottery, writing or fashion design. Your ability to take on your surroundings also means that you're a brilliant actor and mimic, so when you make a character study, you become the person you are focusing on. You'll feel at home in any job that can use your extraordinarily rich imagination and when your mind's in creative flow, it feels like you left a hundred tabs open on your internet browser. Visual ideas appear to download themselves into your mind from an invisible intergalactic portal.

The feet are associated with Pisces, and your graceful versatility might draw you to a career as a dancer, gymnast or ice-skater, and working in the charity sector affords you the opportunity to use your empathy and compassion for a good cause. If you feel you're making a difference to other people's lives, you'll probably stick around in that pond for years to come.

FISH AT THE TOP

You're an even-tempered, slightly reclusive boss and responsibility can sit uneasily on your shoulders. Unless you have a smattering of workaholic Capricorn or Virgo in your chart – people come first. If someone on your team is sick or has to lend a hand in a family drama, you'll usher them out the door yourself, with instructions for bedrest or sincere wishes for their cat's welfare. And you live by the same rules. If someone needs you, they're your priority.

You are connected very closely to your team and your mood will often change, reflecting the demeanour of the group as a whole. Just by walking past your team you can sense if there's something they're not telling you – and sometimes you would rather not know what that is!

Periods of self-employment can prove a wonderful way to improve your self-discipline, as you'll have no choice but to stick to schedules and deadlines. You have a love-hate relationship with money, but when you're your own boss, procrastination no longer becomes an option when you have to keep on top of your own invoices.

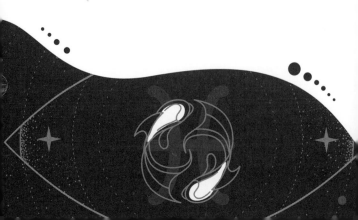

Most compatible colleagues

Aquarius – these guys love working with your brilliant imagination and they can add an ingenious, inventive touch that makes your ideas sing.

Capricorn – you work well with these quiet, hardworking types, and they respect your need to be left to your own devices.

Gemini – you both live in your heads, and you can take any Gemini idea and visualise it into something spectacular – and they never run out of inspiring thoughts.

Least compatible colleagues

Sagittarius – you'll have to make a big noise to grab the attention of Sagittarius, so you'd rather they just left you in peace to get on with looking after the future of humanity.

Libra – they can't make up their mind and you can be disorganised ... It's a distracting mix that rarely comes up with a solid plan.

Cancer – you're both good friends, but at work the pair of you are so woolly together that neither of you is completely sure what the other is meant to be doing.

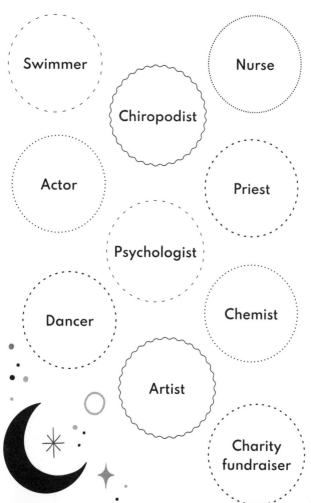

Perfect
Pisces Careers

Swimmer

Nurse

Chiropodist

Actor

Priest

Psychologist

Dancer

Chemist

Artist

Charity fundraiser

HELPING THE REST
OF HUMANITY
IS THE ONLY
POSSIBLE WAY TO
HELP MYSELF.

Pisces friends and family

*Y*ou are a devoted, kind and compassionate friend who probably has a few friendships going back to at least school days. As a deeply compassionate person, you bend over backwards to make your friends, family, neighbours – and complete strangers – feel happy and cared for. You're strongly compelled to relieve suffering, and with such a giving nature you're often found volunteering at your neighbourhood homeless shelter, organising litter-picking sessions, or adopting stray dogs and cats. You're quite a shy individual but your intensely giving nature often sees you finding new friends at your many philanthropic ventures or at the local church, meditation circle, or psychic group.

Your willingness to help can sometimes see others take advantage of your good nature, but you're so shocked at others' selfish motives, that if you feel someone has taken you for granted, you'll swim as far away from them as possible, never to be seen again.

ASTONISHING INTUITION

Non-judgmental and a brilliant listener, you have an almost psychic ability to feel others' emotions, so you're right there with them through the happy or sad times.

You appear to be linked in to invisible sources, and can sense when something is amiss, and as you often can't articulate exactly what, or use logic alone, to get your message through to the people you care about, you may instead quietly prepare to do what you can for them in anticipation of their world going pear-shaped.

You give without asking anything in return, and the people in your life come way before any practical concern, including being on time for work, or eating regular meals. You're also unusually generous with money, which can leave you out of pocket when you really need it. You selflessly put yourself second – and sometimes third or fourth – but you soon learn that to have the energy to look out for everyone else, you need to make your own well-being a top priority.

PISCES AT HOME

Whether it's a metaphorical goldfish bowl or a luminous aquarium, your home will be tranquil and mysterious, with shimmering fabrics and reflective glass or crystal touches. Favouring blues, greens and iridescent splashes in your decor, with sea-themed photography prints, ornaments, and shells. A little chaotic by nature, your clutter seems to blend in with the rest of your possessions and after a while you don't notice the difference! It's not that you're disorganised, you just like to have everything on show. Stuffed with art gear, musical instruments, sewing stuff and half-finished craft projects, your home's separate rooms blend into each other as one large creative, glittery, glory hole. Throw in a few stray cats and dogs, and a couple of pals looking for a sofa for the night and you'll have a Pisces paradise.

PISCES PARENT

Pisces parents will do most anything for their children. You know how to appeal to little kids' sense of wonder without ever needing a television or a computer game as your storytelling is so vivid and believable. You can create whole worlds to inhabit, and you're almost as fond of them as your little ones are. At times a little absent-minded and detached, you can be forgetful about life's practicalities, such as laundry, regular dinner times or boring school homework, but who needs those when you have an imaginative Pisces around?

PISCES CHILD

Sensitive and thoughtful Pisces children often have a faraway look in their eyes, as if they're connected to the Moon or perhaps remembering a past life. Their boundless imagination can keep them entertained for hours and they'll live in their favourite books and create magical worlds with just chewing gum and string.

Healthy Pisces

*G*raceful, delicate and a little shy, as an emotional Water sign, you usually exist inside your emotions and your imagination. Ruled by magical but confusing Neptune, you may start off with good intentions about losing weight or exercising, but you become disillusioned when you don't see fast results.

Your imagination can be the most active thing about you, and because you're such a visual person, creating a mood board with images of people or clothes you like the look of, will help you keep on track. You might feel too self-conscious exercising in a group environment, or mortified by a personal trainer's close scrutiny, so going it alone at home or joining an internet class – with your camera off – should keep things more private.

Dancing is a much-loved Pisces activity, as it's linked with the feet – the Piscean area of the body. Like a fish shimmying through water, you're an elegant, gliding mover, and appreciate the finer aspects of dance which can be lost on the Earth and Fire zodiac signs. And, of course, you're literally right in your element swimming and being in the water and going for a quick dip in the ocean can feel like a religious experience.

FOOD AND DRINK

If you're feeling stressed or anxious you can absent-mindedly use food as a way to stop you from focusing on what is really bothering you. You might even binge eat – and drink – to level out your changeable moods. And as far as you're concerned, it doesn't matter if the glass is half-full or half-empty, there's still plenty of room for wine!

Your first instincts when not feeling great are usually Neptunian – and therefore escapist in nature. Turning to alcohol, chocolate or any mood-altering substance might work for a while, but unfortunately most of the addictive things in life aren't very good for you. Luckily there are other, more satisfying, ways to escape … meditation, sex, even losing yourself in an amazing book, or singing in a choir will all help you rise above your mundane existence for long enough to make you feel part of something more beautiful again.

BODY AND SOUL

Another way to make sure you're firmly rooted in the here and now is to treat emotional issues as seriously as you do physical ones. Seeking counselling or emotional therapy will make you much more aware of any escapist tendencies and will help you stay grounded and present. Otherwise you can feel like a fish out of water and become irritated with your environment, making you prone to allergies, sensitive skin and sometimes asthma or chest tightness.

BODY AREA: FEET

Just as you are the last sign of the zodiac, Pisces is associated with the last body area: the feet. Piscean feet are usually remarkable, perhaps fine-boned and delicate or large and pale; you could think of them as being fin-like. Pisces often have a large collection of exquisite footwear. You might be more prone to foot trouble than most, so try not to ignore any little niggling problems as they could turn into more annoying problems.

Pisces on the move

*T*ime spent away from your usual routines is incredibly important to you, as you long to escape from the everyday world and travel gives you the perfect, legitimate, excuse to do just that. When you need to get away, you're looking to completely relax and recover from the daily grind. You like to plan a trip with plenty of time to spare so you can daydream about what you might do with your time off, or to look forward to just chilling out.

GET PACKING

Packing for your trip is an enjoyable task as you'll probably own a few unique 'just for holiday' items: a beach towel with sentimental value, a gorgeous, floaty sarong that only comes out for special occasions, or a glamorous summer hat that reminds you of when you met your first love. As the zodiac sign most connected with photography, packing a decent camera is essential, and you'll be sure to remember some good books and music to catch up on too. You're not the most self-disciplined person, so if you need to be at an airport or train station at a particular time, perhaps ask a friend to call you up and yell at you, just in case you sleep through your alarm.

ARTY CITIES OR DISNEY?

You're quite swept off your feet by beautiful surroundings: peaceful beaches, sweet-smelling woods and tranquil lake settings, but you also see your time off as a chance to catch up with what's going on in the art world and will be drawn towards vibrant places famed for their passion for film, art, photography, music, dance and literature. Barcelona, Paris and Rome would provide a treasure-trove of cultural marvels that will hook your imagination off to somewhere wonderful. If you're traveling with family, waterslide or amusement parks will take your mind off any worries, stimulate your imagination, and tickle your senses. The pure fantasy of Disneyworld or any sea-themed fantastical attraction will provide welcome fun and distraction. You could blow your budget on a glamorous cruise of a lifetime, allowing the ocean to rejuvenate your senses while you explore fabulous locations while still being able to retreat to a luxurious cabin whenever you choose.

CHURCH OR BEACH?

There are many different kinds of beach setting that will soothe your soul. If it's a tranquil outlook you're dreaming of, let the days melt into each other while you snooze in a hammock over a bath-warm, turquoise sea on a remote Thai island. But you don't have to get exotic to be at one with the waves – a romantic beach picnic with your partner on any local beach will feel like you've been away for a weekend.

A cheap and cheerful beach holiday in Spain is fine, as long as whoever you're travelling with doesn't mind leaving you in a deckchair with a good book and a pina colada.

The most spiritual sign of the zodiac, you feel a special kind of reverence visiting churches or religious landmarks, not only for the metaphysical experience but also to admire their fascinating historic beauty. Ancient spiritual places such as Stonehenge, Nasir al-Mulk Mosque in Iran or the Camino de Santiago pilgrimage route in Spain are some of your favourite destinations on the planet.

YOUR KIND OF PLACE

For a mind-blowingly Piscean adventure, you'll literally be in your element in watery, romantic Venice with its awe-inspiring architecture and renaissance art. And when you've had your fill of Venice's cultural delights, head to the Lido – a beach strip island that's only a 15-minute boat trip from the centre of town, famous for hosting the Venice International Film Festival.

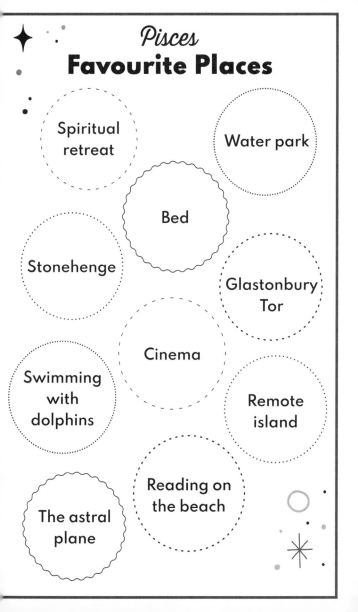

Pisces
Travel Ethic

WE NEED TO
NOURISH OUR
SOULS AS WELL AS
OUR BODIES ON
HOLIDAY.

Pisces
BIRTHDATE
PERSONALITIES

Discover your personal forecast for the day of your birth.

20 February

*Y*ou are a caring and capable person with both an awareness and a deep sensitivity to others' feelings. You desire to be of service and inspire people to enjoy life. With your vivid imagination and the practical ability to translate your ideas into material results, you do well in any artistic ventures. You are warm and tactile and people feel at ease in your company. Partnerships are essential to you, and yet can let you down. Romantically you are looking for an ideal which doesn't exist. You need a partner who showers you with affection, and yet you are never satisfied. What you are seeking is spiritual solace, and that connection comes when you give to others. Charity work can appeal to you and volunteering at a homeless shelter would be richly rewarding.

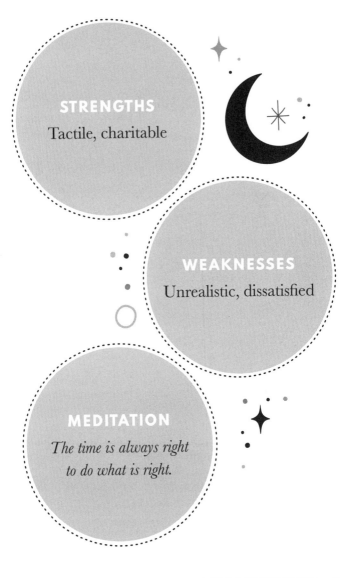

STRENGTHS
Tactile, charitable

WEAKNESSES
Unrealistic, dissatisfied

MEDITATION
*The time is always right
to do what is right.*

21 February

*Y*ou are a humorous and highly intelligent person with a great sense of fun. A brilliant mimic with a love of words and images, you are a natural actor or screen-writer. Whatever you do, it absorbs you totally and your mind works overtime. You have a fertile imagination and are extremely talkative, loving to discuss your work with anyone who cares to listen. Although you are very sociable, you can also be shy and nervous. Your biggest gift is the ability to inspire magic in people, but you also have a tendency to daydream and be caught up in fanciful, impractical projects. You enjoy the good things in life but are not fervent about getting ahead financially. In love, you are tender and playful and need to be on the same wavelength as your partner. Going to a movie allows you escape your mental chatter.

STRENGTHS

Humorous,
imaginative,
affectionate

WEAKNESSES

Shy and impractical

MEDITATION

*If you believe you can,
you probably can.*

22 February

*Y*ou are a compassionate and thoughtful person who is very warm and generous. Extremely emotional, you are always in touch with your feelings. You know instinctively what people are feeling and they can count on you for comfort and a sympathetic ear. Helping others is your raison d'être and you would make a superb therapist, minister of religion, or healer. Your biggest weakness is your extreme sensitivity, and you can be offended by the slightest thing. In relationships you come alive, and an appreciative partner can help you flourish. Domestic life suits you and you are content to play the parental role. Living and being by water is a priority, so installing a water feature – such as a waterfall or pond in your garden – relaxes you and restores your well-being.

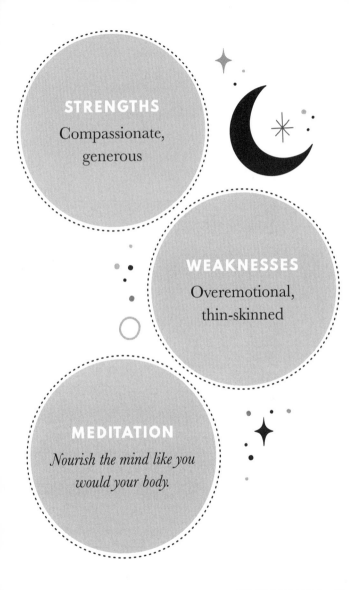

STRENGTHS
Compassionate,
generous

WEAKNESSES
Overemotional,
thin-skinned

MEDITATION
*Nourish the mind like you
would your body.*

23 February

*Y*ou are a gloriously confident and loving person. Totally immersed in discovering yourself, you are a dreamer and creator of a magical life; you seem to have the Midas touch. You have the gift of playfulness and people feel young and alive in your company. Always drawn to centre-stage, the worlds of theatre, television or the movies beckon. You need others' admiration and applause to feel validated. However, you are easily upset and need to retreat to lick your wounds if someone criticizes you. Reaching out to help others by entertaining them is the perfect solution. You cherish your illusions and seek to make them come true. In love you shine, every cell of your being vibrates with joy. You need a partner who is faithful as you can't bear competition.

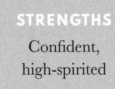

STRENGTHS
Confident,
high-spirited

WEAKNESSES
Vulnerable,
attention-craving

MEDITATION
*Convince yourself that
you have no limits.*

24 February

*Y*ou are a devoted and thoughtful person. You have a rich imagination combined with a practical and methodical mind. Your abilities are profound as you are able to access the wider picture through your intuition and psychic powers and bring your vision into manifestation. Attracted to healing as a profession, you are caring and sensitive in your approach so would make an ideal counsellor or health practitioner. Concerned about nutrition, a vegetarian or macrobiotic diet has great appeal. Your health is vulnerable as you have a tendency to get anxious over the tiniest of things. In relationships, you can fall in love with a fantasy, so you need to make sure you truly know someone before committing. When you find the right person your nurturing side blossoms and you are a gentle and affectionate partner.

STRENGTHS

Caring, imaginative

WEAKNESSES

Worrier, fanciful

MEDITATION

*Winning isn't everything,
but wanting to win is.*

25 February

*Y*ou are a cultured and charming person with a love of beauty and harmony. With a clear, balanced mind and a gift of eloquence, you are a natural diplomat and peacemaker. Love is all-important for you and your relationships are an integral part of your life. People can let you down as you have unrealistic ideals and in business and personal life you need to manage your expectations. Your creativity is an expression of your love and you make a mesmerizing dancer or actor. People can feel transported to another realm through your art. Once you recognize that your need for love can only be filled by a connection with the divine, your relationships dramatically improve. A tear-jerker movie is your idea of a great night out, as it gives you the opportunity to feel your emotions.

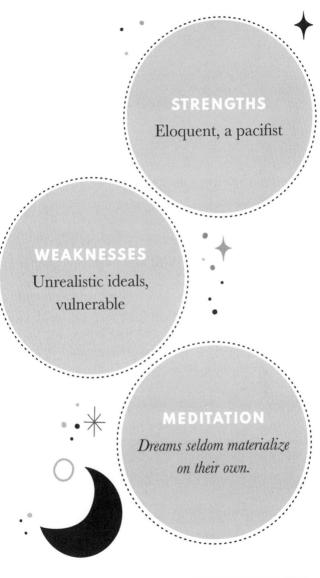

STRENGTHS
Eloquent, a pacifist

WEAKNESSES
Unrealistic ideals,
vulnerable

MEDITATION
*Dreams seldom materialize
on their own.*

26 February

*Y*ou are an emotionally complex person with tremendous courage and determination. Your life has an epic quality to it; a story of agony and ecstasy. Highly emotional and willing to face the depths of your being, you prefer time alone when you can analyse and sort yourself out. This 'cave' is vital for you, but you can get trapped in self-absorption. Your fascination with emotions, together with a brilliant intellect, can lead you into a career as a psychoanalyst or medical researcher. All of your relationships are eventful, and your passion and intensity can flare up or down – your partner is in for a turbulent time. However, you are the most exciting lover and no one can ever accuse you of being boring! A night out at a rock concert allows you to release all that excess energy.

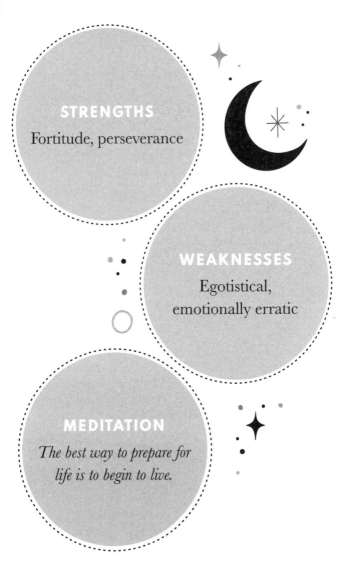

STRENGTHS

Fortitude, perseverance

WEAKNESSES

Egotistical,
emotionally erratic

MEDITATION

*The best way to prepare for
life is to begin to live.*

27 February

*Y*ou are an intensely passionate and fiery person with a generous heart. A seeker of truth, you are attracted to higher education and philosophy. Deeply spiritual, you tend to avoid the conventional religions of your native country, experimenting with those of a foreign culture. You are able to find meaning in the tragic and negative situations in life. As a creative person with 'big picture' mentality, you need a lot of freedom to explore and move around. Movies are an ideal career path for you, especially directing. The roles of therapist or teacher are also suitable. In relationships, you are very open and giving, but you have high expectations. You can be deeply disappointed in love, and easily get caught sacrificing things you love which leads to resentment. Being actively involved with an overseas charity helps you to rise above everyday problems.

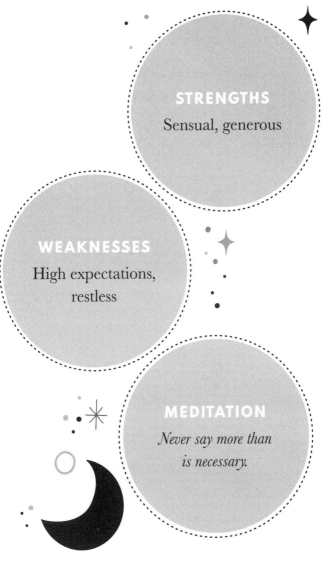

STRENGTHS
Sensual, generous

WEAKNESSES
High expectations,
restless

MEDITATION
*Never say more than
is necessary.*

28 February

*Y*ou are an empathic and resourceful person with a combination of common sense and imagination. Not overtly ambitious, you are content to work behind the scenes. Your intuitive gifts make you very popular as you know what people need and can give it to them. This talent makes you an ideal composer, architect or set designer. You love a challenge and are an excellent organizer. As you are deeply caring and can inspire people, you also make a great fundraiser. When you fall in love you can be secretive and shy and keep your feelings hidden. Once you decide on your perfect mate – which can take some time as you have very high standards and expectations – you are faithful and loyal. You love a spectacle so a night at a sound-and-light show would be heaven for you.

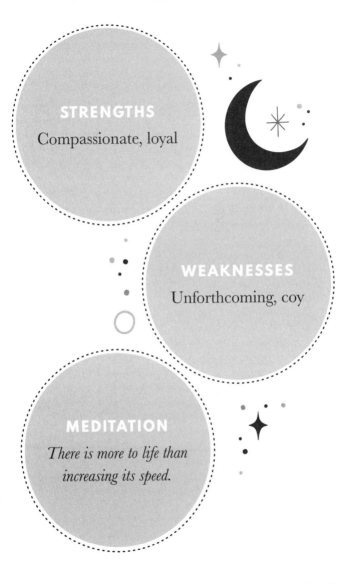

STRENGTHS
Compassionate, loyal

WEAKNESSES
Unforthcoming, coy

MEDITATION
There is more to life than increasing its speed.

29 February

*Y*ou are a trustworthy and progressive person who is very much the humanitarian. There is an edgy quality to you and a hint of danger, which is very exciting. An idealist, you dream of a better world where equality and freedom exists for everyone. You have respect for the rules of society, yet also push the boundaries. A born campaigner for social reform, politics is a natural career path. However, you can get on your soapbox and come across as hectoring others. Your saving grace is your quirky sense of humour. In relationships, you need a lot of time on your own and can be emotionally reserved. Yet under your cool exterior you are tender and devoted. Playing a team game such as cricket or baseball is wonderful for you, as you delight in the camaraderie.

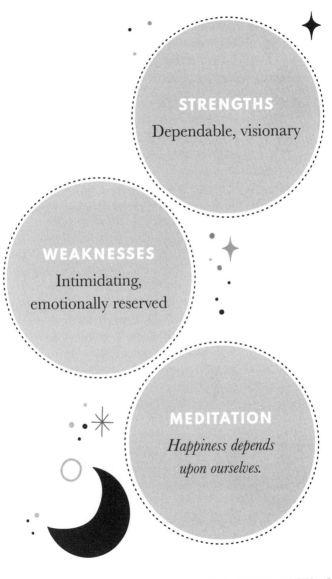

STRENGTHS
Dependable, visionary

WEAKNESSES
Intimidating,
emotionally reserved

MEDITATION
*Happiness depends
upon ourselves.*

1 March

*Y*ou are a warm and optimistic person with a soft and sentimental heart. Extremely gifted, especially at music, you have the imagination and the initiative to be a pioneer. You think on your feet, but can be impetuous and rush ahead without considering all the angles, much to the chagrin of others. With your courage and compassion you do well when actively helping others, especially if travel is an essential part of the job. You are not afraid to speak your mind, but can have a reputation for being temperamental. This comes from an inner fear of not being recognized for your abilities. A loving relationship will go a long to way helping you find balance in your life. You fall in love easily, and are very romantic. An active sport that lets you express all your frustrations such as rally driving is perfect.

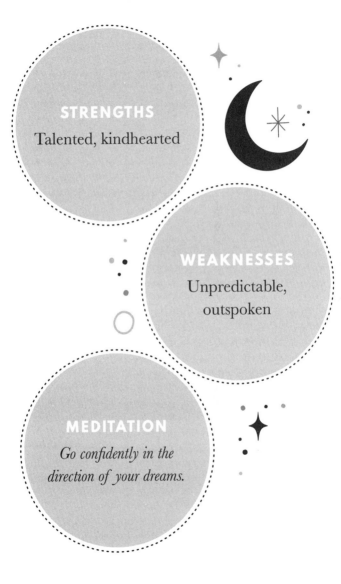

STRENGTHS

Talented, kindhearted

WEAKNESSES

Unpredictable,
outspoken

MEDITATION

*Go confidently in the
direction of your dreams.*

2 March

*Y*ou are a sweet-tempered and affectionate person with a love of the simple
pleasures in life. Extremely sensuous,
you adore the sights, smells and sounds of
nature and are happiest in the countryside.
You need to put down roots so your creativity
can blossom. Cooking is a fabulous experience
for you and you present food as an art form.
Entertaining groups of people is your forte
and you are sensitive to their needs, so a career
in public relations is excellent. You have an
ability to be content, but need to be careful
not to become lazy or overindulge your sweet
tooth. Romance is never far from your mind
and you are a delightful and thoughtful lover.
Your weakness is being overly possessive. Trust
is an important lesson for you. Relax and tend
to your garden.

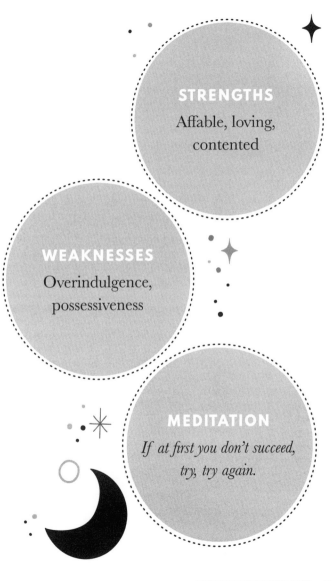

STRENGTHS
Affable, loving,
contented

WEAKNESSES
Overindulgence,
possessiveness

MEDITATION
*If at first you don't succeed,
try, try again.*

3 March

*Y*ou are a curious and highly articulate person with a youthful air about you. Connected totally to your inner dream world, ideas come to you in a flash and you can't help but share them with everyone. A born communicator and natural filmmaker, you are attracted to television and the internet in particular for its immediacy. With a delightful, lighthearted sense of humour, you are quixotic and almost fairylike in your energy. Children just adore you because they sense that you are still a child at heart. In relationships, you need a lot of space and variety and can't bear to feel hemmed in. Your restlessness can result in you being fickle. However, you can also become dependent on your partner to give you the stability you need. Dancing freestyle is wonderful for you to express your individuality.

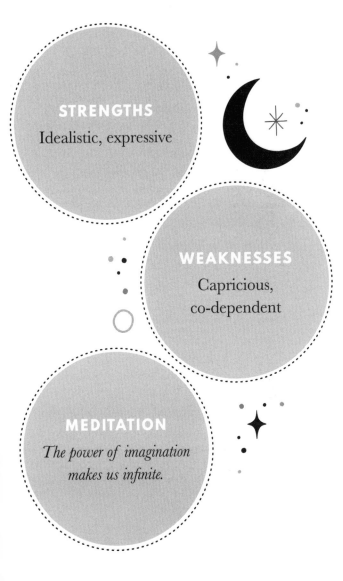

STRENGTHS
Idealistic, expressive

WEAKNESSES
Capricious,
co-dependent

MEDITATION
*The power of imagination
makes us infinite.*

4 March

*Y*ou are a versatile and sensitive person with a colourful imagination. Artistically gifted, your ability to touch people's deepest feelings with your creativity can make you a well-known and loved artist. Candidly photographing or painting people is your strength as you can capture emotion brilliantly. Plus, you are quiet and unobtrusive so they never know you're there and you seldom offend. You wear your heart on your sleeve and can be moody and ultra-emotional, veering on high drama. To overcome this is a challenge, and channelling your feelings into an artistic project is the perfect solution. When you fall in love you commit wholeheartedly as you long for a family and tend to marry young. Being with loved ones changes you for the better and this is when your zany sense of humour comes out to play.

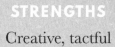

STRENGTHS

Creative, tactful

WEAKNESSES

Overdramatic,
temperamental

MEDITATION

*Discontent is the source
of all trouble.*

5 March

*Y*ou are an articulate and fiery person with a flair for the dramatic. Warm and friendly, you offer encouragement and inspiration to all. You need to be respected and admired, so seek a leadership position in whatever field you enter. Your talents are spectacular either as a musician, actor, or in business. Taking the lead is natural, however, you are sensitive to what people think of you and need constant reassurance. From time to time your moodiness and self-pity get the better of you and you become withdrawn. Then you are liable to create a dramatic scene just so people pay attention! With a vivid imagination and love of fantasy, you love being in love and express your whole heart as the most romantic and tender of lovers. Watching the sunset touches the essence of you and reconnects you to your source.

STRENGTHS

Encouraging, expressive

WEAKNESSES

Volatile and, at times, reticent

MEDITATION

What you dislike in another take care to correct in yourself.

6 March

*Y*ou are an adaptable and discerning person with a soft and shy nature. Artistically talented, your vivid imagination plays an important role in your career choice. Your music and poetry can inspire others to a state of transcendence. You have a 'feel' for things and act on your hunches and are also able to pay great attention to detail. These abilities make you a success in business as you have an uncanny knack of knowing when to take risks. However, you are a daydreamer and sometimes want to escape, so you can be prone to addictions. As you become materially successful, you become philanthropic and give generously of your time and money to help others. In relationships, you need a partner who keeps up with your ever-changing interests. You are a bit of a softy and need to feel cared for.

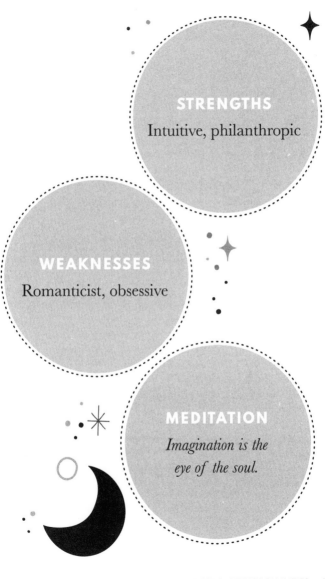

STRENGTHS

Intuitive, philanthropic

WEAKNESSES

Romanticist, obsessive

MEDITATION

*Imagination is the
eye of the soul.*

7 March

*Y*ou are a gracious and gentle person with an ethereal and entrancing quality. You love glamour and beauty and are attracted to the art world, photography and the theatre. With your delicacy of touch and elegant good taste you are also at home in the fashion business. Wherever you work it has to be aesthetically pleasing as ugliness is abhorrent to you. With a dignified manner and charm you are the perfect host as you can make everyone feel at ease. A weakness is your indecisiveness as you want to please people and keep everyone happy. In your personal relationship you can be 'in love with love' and can't bear to be alone so can cling on to a bad relationship. Romance is your lifeblood so an intimate candlelight dinner followed by dancing feeds your soul.

STRENGTHS
Accommodating,
honourable

WEAKNESSES
Indecisive, a people
pleaser

MEDITATION
*Smile, it makes a world
of difference.*

8 March

*Y*ou are an extraordinary person with a quiet yet powerful strength and captivating manner. Never superficial, highly intuitive and emotionally courageous, you are a person who doesn't flinch from facing the darker sides of life. With an intellectual and analytical mind, you are fascinated by exploring reincarnation, the ancient wisdom traditions and metaphysics. Maths, computing, politics or biology are more traditional career options. Your weakness is that you can be overly-suspicious of people's motives. In relationships, you need a lot of love and are very vulnerable. This can result in you being very jealous and possessive. With maturity, and over time, you can relax and trust your partner. You need excitement and passion and the opera or a murder mystery is the perfect escape from reality.

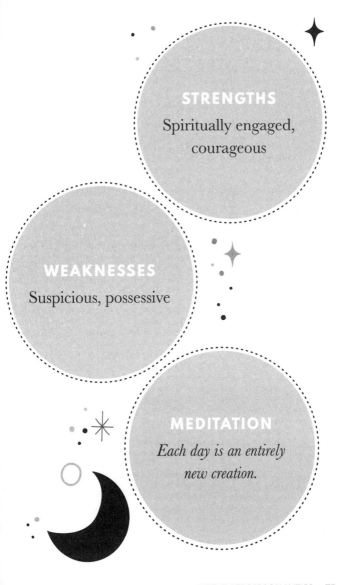

STRENGTHS

Spiritually engaged,
courageous

WEAKNESSES

Suspicious, possessive

MEDITATION

*Each day is an entirely
new creation.*

9 March

*Y*ou are an exuberant and generous person who is always looking for a new adventure. You adore travel and seek to constantly expand your mind with books, films and the internet. The life of an explorer or philosopher is definitely one for you. However, you are never satisfied with sticking to one thing, lack focus and can get overwhelmed by all your projects and end up achieving very little. You have an endearing naivety and can make people laugh, so everyone wants to be your friend. They are astounded by your optimism and positive outlook. In love you are affectionate and enjoy companionship, but get itchy feet and can only be happy with someone who understands your need for freedom. Hiking is one sport you enjoy, especially along the coastline or by lakes.

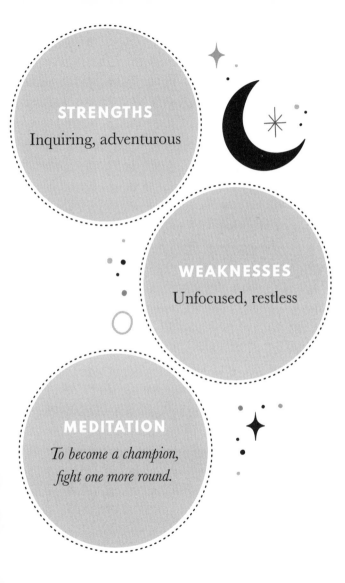

STRENGTHS

Inquiring, adventurous

WEAKNESSES

Unfocused, restless

MEDITATION

*To become a champion,
fight one more round.*

10 March

*Y*ou are a cautious yet charitable person with genuine kindness. You have a deep sense of duty and are traditional in your outlook, with good old-fashioned values. With shrewd perception and compassion, plus an awareness of people's emotions, you are a talented psychologist or counsellor. However, you have a tendency to take on others' burdens in your desire to be helpful, which can lead to burnout. You are prone to worry and pessimism, so finding a spiritual or religious path is vital for your long-term wellbeing. In your relationships, you thrive on intimacy but also desire security and will take your time seeking a partner who can give you that. You love your family yet are also self-sufficient. A sport that is really you is ice-skating; romance and discipline combined. Perfect!

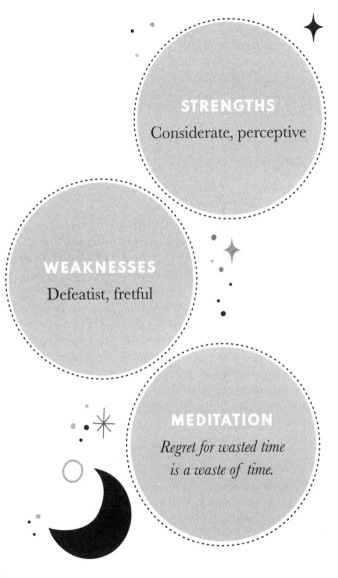

STRENGTHS
Considerate, perceptive

WEAKNESSES
Defeatist, fretful

MEDITATION
*Regret for wasted time
is a waste of time.*

11 March

*Y*ou are a brilliantly inventive person who is usually way ahead of their time. You are not afraid to experiment and come up with whacky and original ideas. As a storyteller you are second to none, and can take people on a magical mystery adventure. The wondrous world of science fiction is your speciality. You are both a scientist and an artist; someone who can use both their left and right brain, which is a rare combination. You are incredibly social and have a wide-ranging circle of friends, some of whom are eccentrics and oddballs. In your romantic relationships, you are loyal and devoted and require a strong intellectual connection. However, you need to spend time alone, so can appear emotionally distant and cool. For total relaxation and entertainment, you appreciate a witty, satirical comedy show.

STRENGTHS

Avant-garde,
imaginative

WEAKNESSES

Unforthcoming, aloof

MEDITATION

*Anger is never without
a reason, but seldom
a good one.*

12 March

You are an unworldly, impressionable person who is extremely altruistic. You are so sensitive that it's as if you have no skin, so you have to develop a protective layer around you. You have an elusive and mystical quality about you and can be hard to pin down. As you get older its easier for you to get in touch with, and draw on, the extraordinary psychic and artistic gifts that you have. Helping others comes easily to you, and you're the one who volunteers to run the homeless shelter or local stray cats' home. In relationships, you can get caught in fantasy and suffer from unrequited love; you have difficulty maintaining permanence in your romantic life. A down-to-earth type is what you need. The opera was invented just for you – it's a memorable night out that will have a long-lasting effect.

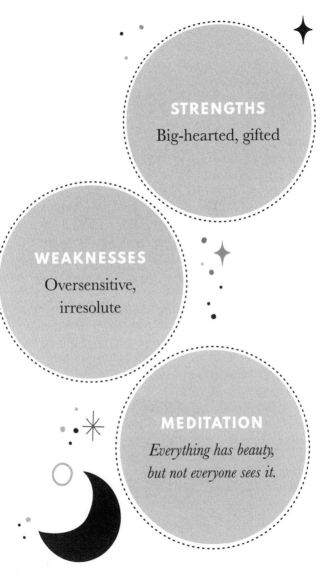

STRENGTHS
Big-hearted, gifted

WEAKNESSES
Oversensitive,
irresolute

MEDITATION
*Everything has beauty,
but not everyone sees it.*

13 March

Y ou are a caring and kind person who is a born romantic. You have a quiet enigmatic quality that is very alluring. Totally aware of your feelings, you can ride an emotional roller coaster at times and soon learn to protect yourself from harsh environments. You have an excellent memory and a gift for listening; talents which make you an imaginative writer, poet or lyricist. You are trustworthy and able to keep secrets; the ideal best friend. With a decidedly theatrical leaning, you would also make a brilliant set designer. In relationships, you need to be careful not to become the doormat as you are incredibly giving to others and tend to neglect your own needs. You tend to pick up any infection going, so you need to support your immune system and detox on a regular basis.

STRENGTHS

Good listener,
trustworthy

WEAKNESSES

Emotionally unstable,
neglectful of personal
needs

MEDITATION

Hope is grief's best music.

14 March

*Y*ou are a person with natural charisma. A great actor, you can exude confidence and charm, enlivening all you meet. No one can question the enormous creative and leadership gifts you possess. However, underneath there is a shy and brooding persona, and you can be racked with self-doubt. These moods can suddenly descend, much to the chagrin of colleagues and loved ones. You have a soft and generous heart and working in the public sector in a leadership position is suited. The stage also whispers seductively, as being in the spotlight is your natural habitat. Relationships are your life and you relish all types of emotion, so heartbreak, dramatic break-ups and passion make you feel alive. Hot saunas match your temperament, as do beach holidays in tropical parts of the world.

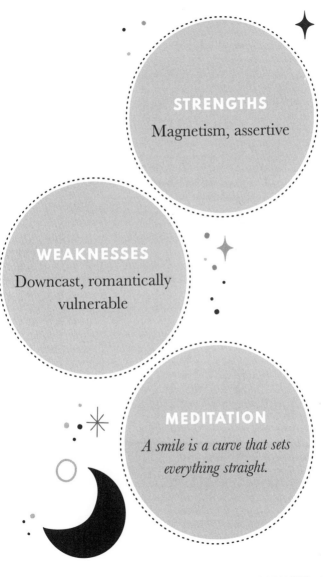

STRENGTHS
Magnetism, assertive

WEAKNESSES
Downcast, romantically
vulnerable

MEDITATION
*A smile is a curve that sets
everything straight.*

15 March

*Y*ou are a sentimental and affectionate person with a healing touch. Reiki, massage and shiatsu are all modalities you might explore as a career. You have the rare knack of combining perceptive insights with practical and efficient solutions. There is a strong desire in you to serve others and you're the ideal person to do voluntary work overseas. At times you can become fretful and uptight about getting everything perfect. This can affect your digestive system so the occasional detox would do you the world of good. Letting go of minor details and working as part of a team would be highly beneficial. In relationships, your partner can get confused as you can drift off one minute and be efficient and attentive the next. Your sense of humour and ability to laugh at yourself saves the day.

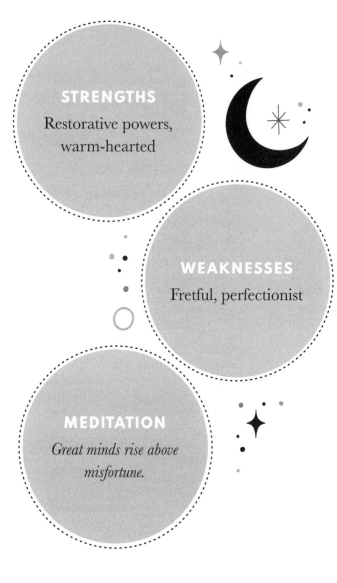

STRENGTHS

Restorative powers,
warm-hearted

WEAKNESSES

Fretful, perfectionist

MEDITATION

*Great minds rise above
misfortune.*

16 March

*Y*ou are an artistic and easy-going person who is inspired by a love of truth. Your soul is that of a poet or mystic and you have a deeply sympathetic and agreeable nature. People adore being around you as you create an enchanted fairyland world usually only seen in movies. You could be the director or writer of an epic love story and your life is a grand romance. You love giving cocktail parties with a witty and fascinating group, especially arty or literary types. Being in love is so important, you can become dependent on your partner and avoid any form of confrontation as you fear being rejected. Your emotions can overwhelm you which makes you vulnerable to colds and flu. Building up your immune system with vitamins and using flower remedies is very helpful to stop you getting run down.

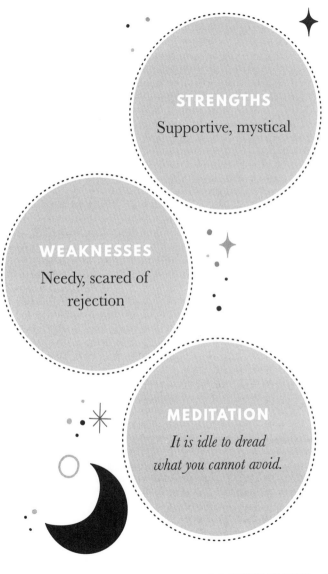

STRENGTHS
Supportive, mystical

WEAKNESSES
Needy, scared of rejection

MEDITATION
*It is idle to dread
what you cannot avoid.*

17 March

*Y*ou are a compassionate and responsive person with a radar for those in trouble that you can help. As a natural healer, your mind focusses on deep subjects, and you are attracted to study psychology, medicine and techniques such as hypnosis. Your motivation is to understand the great mysteries of life and death. Perceptive and dedicated, you can be very successful once you find your niche. When tired you can be cantankerous and scathing, especially of people who underestimate your intelligence – you don't suffer fools gladly. Relationships are the centre of your life and you are fiercely loyal to those you love. You can overflow with feelings and need a partner who can support your emotional nature and ground you. A daily swim or rigorous yoga session is a way to balance you and restore your equilibrium.

STRENGTHS
Receptive and
insightful

WEAKNESSES
Bad-tempered, cutting

MEDITATION
*If you want time,
you must make it.*

18 March

*Y*ou are a benevolent and kind person with a far-ranging imagination. You have a strong sense of moral integrity and are very spiritual, always believing the best in people. With your tender heart you can be gullible and taken in by any sob story, so people can easily deceive you. Career-wise you are creative and extremely versatile so have many options open to you. Choosing just one profession can be difficult, but you need to feel it has meaning and contributes to improving people's lives. In your love affairs you need an intellectual equal and someone who stimulates your fertile imagination. You also need lot of time alone to do your own thing. You favour adventure rather than the conventional holidays – travelling across the desert on a camel has more appeal for you than a beach resort.

STRENGTHS

Imaginative, kind, bounteous

WEAKNESSES

Overtrusting, easily deceived

MEDITATION

Difficulties strengthen the mind.

19 March

*Y*ou are a sympathetic and helpful person who has a strong moral integrity and genuine concern for others. Serious-minded and self-reflective, you have a quiet demeanour that belies an inner core of strength. You are a skilled business person capable of managing large groups as you have acute sensitivity for how people feel. This ability keeps you in tune with the public mood and you would do well in the fashion or movie industry. However, if you do not receive constant appreciation of your efforts, you can become defensive and critical, in order to hide your lack of confidence. In relationships you are romantic and loving and once you commit your word is your bond. You need to lighten up and the ballet is the kind of fantasy world you find delightful.

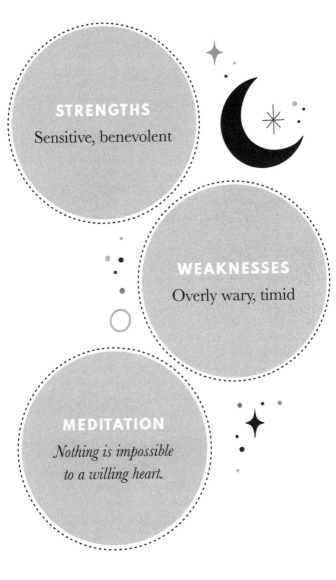

STRENGTHS

Sensitive, benevolent

WEAKNESSES

Overly wary, timid

MEDITATION

*Nothing is impossible
to a willing heart.*

20 March

*Y*ou are a demonstrative and loving person with a huge desire to express yourself creatively. You have a soft and gentle touch and everything you do is imbued with beauty and grace. Whether as a massage therapist, a garden designer or a carpenter, you relish being hands-on in your work and connecting with people. You enjoy life and believe it has to be lived in each moment – you really know how to relax. Totally subjective and with a tendency to be over-emotional, you respond intuitively to any situation. Being logical just isn't your thing. At times you are so changeable that you can drive others to distraction. Being in love is bliss; you blossom as your best qualities emerge. You are quite happy pottering around on your own, and it's important that you let others know this.

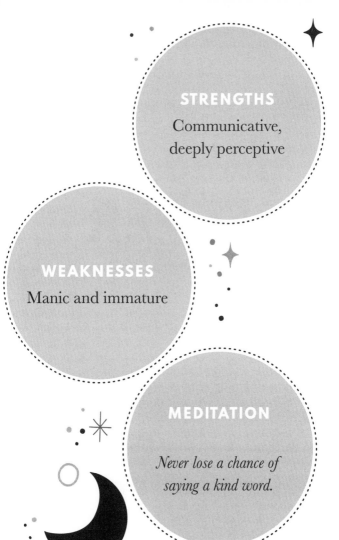

STRENGTHS
Communicative,
deeply perceptive

WEAKNESSES
Manic and immature

MEDITATION
*Never lose a chance of
saying a kind word.*

Going
DEEPER

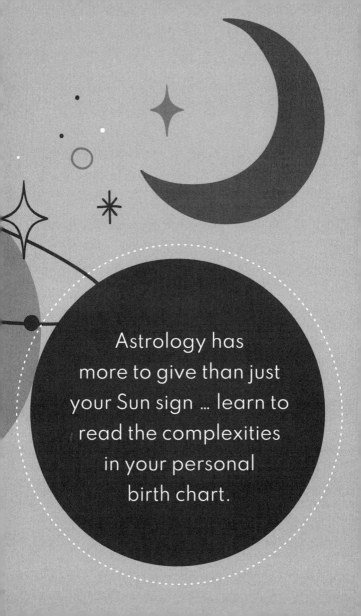

Astrology has more to give than just your Sun sign … learn to read the complexities in your personal birth chart.

Your personal birth chart

*U*nderstanding your Sun sign is an essential part of astrology, but it's the tip of the iceberg. To take your astrological wisdom to the next level, you'll need a copy of your unique birth chart – a map of the heavens for the precise moment you were born. You can find your birth chart at the Free Horoscopes link at: www.astro.com.

ASTROLOGICAL SYNTHESIS

When you first explore your chart you'll find that as well as a Sun sign, you also have a Moon sign, plus a Mercury, Venus, Mars, Jupiter, Saturn, Neptune, Uranus and Pluto sign – and that they all mean something different. Then there's astrological houses to consider, ruling planets and Rising signs, aspects and element types – all of which you will learn more about in the birth chart section on pages 112–115.

The art to astrology is in synthesising all this intriguing information to paint a picture of someone's character, layer by layer. Now that you understand your Pisces Sun personality better, it's time to go deeper, and to look at the next layer – your Moon sign. To find out more about your own Moon sign go to pages 104–111.

THE MOON'S INFLUENCE

After the Sun, your Moon sign is the second biggest astrological influence in your birth chart. It describes your emotional nature – your feelings, instincts and moods and how you respond to different sorts of people and situations. By blending your outer, Pisces Sun character with your inner, emotional, Moon sign, you'll get a much more balanced picture. If you don't feel that you're 100% Pisces, your Moon sign will probably explain why!

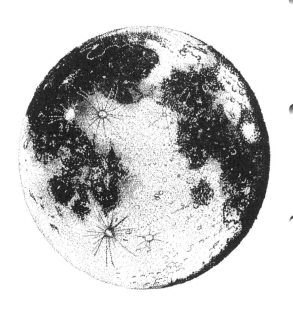

Pisces with Moon signs

PISCES SUN/**ARIES MOON**

 Your strong Aries Moon is in stark contrast to your gentle Pisces Sun. Aries is a warrior who wants to lead and stand out in a crowd, which is an interesting contrast with your Pisces Sun, which prefers to stand back and take the line of least resistance. Your self-belief is strong and your empathy for people who are struggling is strong. You have a protective instinct over your loved ones and will stick up for yourself in any challenging situations. You're passionate and romantic, with an intense inner world, a mixture of hot-headed Mars and your deep Neptunian feelings. Your emotional reactions are likely to be strong and immediate, as it's probably difficult for you to keep a lid on things, but you return to a tranquil state as quickly as you blew up.

PISCES SUN/**TAURUS MOON**

 Your Earth Taurus Moon is very grounding for your Pisces Sun and will help you create and build all that your boundless Neptunian imagination can muster.

Taurus Moons are patient and sensible and like to see results, which should act as an anchor for your dreamy, sensitive Sun. Your Venus/Neptune combination loves to create beauty, and you likely have talent as an artist, musician or designer. Taurus gives you a sensible attitude to making money, and will help you to value your own talents, and to spot them in other people. You're a quiet, peace-loving person, calm and rooted, but you have your limits. You're slow to anger, but you're no fool – if you have cause to get angry at someone, they probably really deserve it!

PISCES SUN/**GEMINI MOON**

Your expressive Gemini Moon means you'll likely want to share how you feel with others and your deeply empathic Sun helps you connect with the people around you in a meaningful way. You have an inner restlessness that prevents you from getting stuck in a rut, and your cheerful Mercury-ruled emotions lightens your outlook and keeps you future-focussed. Your thoughts and feelings are changeable, and you adapt easily to changing circumstances. Rarely still for long, you're always curious about what's happening around the next corner. You have a love of travel and find it easy to feel at home in different environments. You enjoy company and finding a partner who is as open and willing to talk about their feelings will be hugely rewarding.

PISCES SUN/**CANCER MOON**

You're so tuned into the feelings of the people around you that you're almost psychic. You're a double Water person, deeply intuitive, sensitive and empathic. Nobody can hide things from you for long because you'll pick up on people's underlying feelings. You live in your fertile imagination and need work that can give you a creative channel. If you don't find a therapeutic outlet you can get snappy with people, which can make you anxious. Working as a caregiver or healer will make you feel needed and valued, and as one of the zodiac's most nurturing personalities you'll also get a kick out of gardening and cooking. As you absorb other people's energies so easily, you need to make sure you get enough sleep, nourishing food and make time for fun with loved ones.

PISCES SUN/**LEO MOON**

You're a warm, empathic person with a flair for the dramatic. A little encouragement goes a long way with you, and you love entertaining and making other people happy. You love children and find it easy to communicate with them, so having a family of your own may be especially important. Teaching comes naturally, and your Pisces Moon gives you the emotional intelligence and nurturing ability to help anyone close to you express how they feel. In relationships you are loyal and giving and enjoy having a partner you can feel proud of. You're generous and spontaneous, which can sometimes have an unstable effect on your bank balance, but you're never that down on your luck because your friends and family are always looking out for you.

PISCES SUN/**VIRGO MOON**

 You're a full Moon baby, born when the Sun and Moon were in opposite signs of the zodiac. Full Moon people often have contradictions in their personality as they try to synthesize very different aspects of their character. Your Virgo Moon is very practical, efficient and organised while your Pisces Sun dislikes having to stick to one set of rules and is more unstructured and poetic in its approach. But both signs are adaptable and fluid, which means you're good in a crisis and you find change quite refreshing. As you are quite self-conscious, you need to watch that you're not being too hard on yourself. As you are so impressionable, you tend to pick up on both positive and negative energy, so you will work best with a partner who is supportive and encouraging.

PISCES SUN/**LIBRA MOON**

 You're a deeply compassionate person, benevolent and fair-minded. Your Libra Moon dislikes being pressured into making decisions because you always want to weigh up all the evidence before judging. And your Pisces Sun is also very sensitive to discord and disharmony, and these two aspects of your personality blend to create a very sensitive soul. You're deeply moved by beauty in all its forms, and colour, photography and film can all have a profound effect on you. You may choose to seek a career that gives you a feeling of structure and security, to give you a sense of permanence, and you crave an emotionally stable partnership as a port in what can feel like a very chaotic world. It's important that you develop some self-assertion, otherwise you may feel thrown around by other people's choices and desires.

PISCES SUN/**SCORPIO MOON**

This is one of the more practical double Water combinations. Your Pisces Sun may seem vague or directionless at times, but your Scorpio Moon usually knows exactly where it's going. You have tremendous reserves of emotional energy, and often have many different passions and interests. You can be a little distrustful of people you don't know well, but once they open up or reveal their inner selves, you quickly warm to them. Attracted to the mysteries of life, you may be fascinated with spirituality and esoteric philosophies. Your Scorpio Moon prefers to keep your own emotions hidden, so that people can't take advantage of your feelings. However, when you fall for someone you are one of the most giving people around.

PISCES SUN/**SAGITTARIUS MOON**

 An open, honest and freedom-loving person, you have an enormous heart and a huge appetite for life. Optimistic and cheerful, you never let life get you down for long. Your intuition is quite remarkable, and you sense what your loved ones want and need from you before they can find the words to articulate themselves. Keenly interested in other people's beliefs, you enjoy travel and meeting people from all walks of life. You can find it difficult to stick to a budget and some financial planning skills would not go amiss as you can be something of an impulsive shopper! A practical partner in love or in business will help you achieve your dreams. With your enthusiasm and imagination, the world is yours for the taking!

PISCES SUN/**CAPRICORN MOON**

 With your ambitious, go-getting Capricorn Moon, your Pisces Sun has stable, strong foundations so that you can freely express your artistic or creative self, knowing you have rules and boundaries. You often set yourself small goals and move towards your desires incrementally, gaining confidence as you go. Your vivid imagination could prove to be a real money spinner, as your Earth-ruled Moon wants to value and make the best of your talents – and you have brilliant intuition when it comes to spotting a potentially lucrative business deal. You're a very alluring mix of quiet determination and emotional intelligence that is very attractive to potential partners. You take life quite seriously, but you have a really off-the-wall sense of humour even in the most challenging circumstances.

PISCES SUN/**AQUARIUS MOON**

 You may have something of an otherworldly vibe. You're compassionate, friendly and caring but with a slightly detached emotional style. Your quirky Aquarian Moon works well with your charitable Pisces Sun, and you are able to connect with, and help, a great many people when you put your mind to it. You've an uncanny knack for sensing where society is headed in the future. Your tech-savvy Aquarius Moon has you tuned into the zeitgeist and you'll be years ahead of your time in some way. You're something of a maverick emotionally, sometimes extremely empathic, sensitive and caring, but erratic, contrary and a little aloof. In relationships you are best suited to someone with many shared interests, as companionship is your number one priority.

PISCES SUN/**PISCES MOON**

 You just have to be in a room with someone to know how they're feeling. You sense other people's emotions more than any other and are linked into a mysterious psychic web of secret, mysterious emotions that other people aren't even aware exists. You're often so lost in your thoughts that it can be a challenge for you to tell the difference between fantasy and reality. It can be tricky for you to take decisive action as you have a chameleon-like ability to adapt to other people and changing circumstances, and sometimes lose a bit of yourself in the process. You're insightful, amiable, incredibly creative, and, although you're a loving partner, family member and friend, you need plenty of time alone to process all your thoughts and feelings.

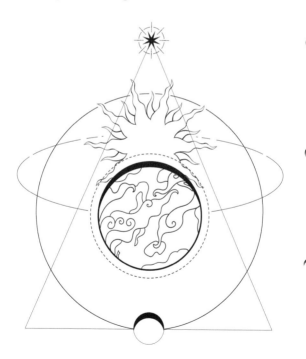

Birth charts

*L*earning about your Sun and Moon sign opens the gateway into exploring your own birth chart. This snapshot of the skies at the moment of birth is as complex and interesting as the person it represents. Astrologers the world over have been studying their own birth charts, and those of people they know, their whole lives and still find something new in them every day. There are many schools of astrology and an inexhaustible list of tools and techniques, but here are the essentials to get you started ...

ZODIAC SIGNS AND PLANETS

These are the keywords for the 12 zodiac signs and the planets associated with them, known as ruling planets.

 ARIES
courageous, bold, aggressive, leading, impulsive

Ruling planet
 MARS
shows where you take action and how you channel your energy

TAURUS
reliable, artistic, practical, stubborn, patient

Ruling planet
VENUS
describes what you value and who and what
you love

GEMINI
clever, friendly, superficial, versatile

Ruling planet
MERCURY
represents how your mind works and how
you communicate

CANCER
emotional, nurturing, defensive, sensitive

Ruling planet
MOON
describes your emotional needs and how you
wish to be nurtured

LEO
confidence, radiant, proud, vain, generous

Ruling planet
SUN
your core personality and character

VIRGO

analytical, organised, meticulous, thrifty

Ruling planet

MERCURY

co-ruler of Gemini and Virgo

LIBRA

fair, indecisive, cooperative, diplomatic

Ruling planet

VENUS

co-ruler of Taurus and Libra

SCORPIO

regenerating, magnetic, obsessive, penetrating

Ruling planet

PLUTO

deep transformation, endings and beginnings

SAGITTARIUS

optimistic, visionary, expansive, blunt, generous

Ruling planet

JUPITER

travel, education and faith in a higher power

CAPRICORN
ambitious, responsible, cautious, conventional

Ruling planet
SATURN
your ambitions, work ethic and restrictions

AQUARIUS
unconventional, independent, erratic, unpredictable

Ruling planet
URANUS
where you rebel or innovate

PISCES
dreamy, chaotic, compassionate, imaginative, idealistic

Ruling planet
NEPTUNE
your unconscious, and where you let things go

The 12 houses

B irth charts are divided into 12 sections, known as houses, each relating to different areas of life as follows:

FIRST HOUSE

associated with *Aries*

Identity – how you appear to others and your initial response to challenges.

SECOND HOUSE

associated with *Taurus*

How you make and spend money, your talents, skills and how you value yourself.

THIRD HOUSE

associated with *Gemini*

Siblings, neighbours, communication and short distance travel.

FOURTH HOUSE

associated with *Cancer*

Home, family, your mother, roots and the past.

FIFTH HOUSE

associated with *Leo*

Love affairs, romance, creativity, gambling and children.

SIXTH HOUSE

associated with *Virgo*

Health, routines,
organisation
and pets.

EIGHTH HOUSE

associated with *Scorpio*

Sex, death,
transformation, wills
and money you share
with another.

SEVENTH HOUSE

associated with *Libra*

Relationships,
partnerships, others
and enemies.

NINTH HOUSE

associated with *Sagittarius*

Travel, education,
religious beliefs, faith
and generosity.

TENTH HOUSE

associated with *Capricorn*

Career, father,
ambitions, worldly
success.

ELEVENTH HOUSE

associated with *Aquarius*

Friends, groups, ideals
and social or political
movements.

TWELFTH HOUSE

associated with *Pisces*

Spirituality, the
unconscious mind,
dreams and
karma.

THE ELEMENTS

Each zodiac sign belongs to one of the four elements – Earth, Air, Fire and Water – and these share similar characteristics, as listed below.

EARTH

Taurus, Virgo, Capricorn

Earth signs are practical, trustworthy, thorough and logical.

AIR

Gemini, Libra, Aquarius

Air signs are clever, flighty, intellectual and charming.

FIRE

Aries, Leo, Sagittarius

Fire signs are active, creative, warm, spontaneous, innovators.

WATER

Cancer, Scorpio, Pisces

Water signs are sensitive, empathic, dramatic and caring.

PLANETARY ASPECTS

The aspects are geometric patterns formed by the planets and represent different types of energy. They are usually shown in two ways – in a separate grid or aspect grid, and as the criss-crossing lines on the chart itself. There are oodles of different aspect patterns but to keep things simple we'll just be working with four: conjunctions, squares, oppositions and trines.

CONJUNCTION

0 degrees apart
intensifying

SQUARE

90 degrees apart
challenging

OPPOSITION

180 degrees apart
polarising

TRINE

120 degrees apart
harmonising

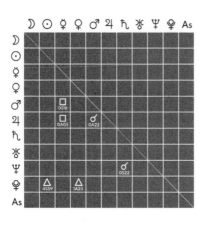

Planetary aspects for Cara's chart

HOUSES AND RISING SIGN

Each chart is a 360° circle, divided into 12 segments known as the houses (see pages 116–117 for house interpretations). The most important point in a birth chart is known as the Rising sign, also known as the Ascendant. This is usually shown as ASC or AS on the chart and it shows the zodiac sign that was rising on the Eastern horizon for the moment you were born. It's always on the middle left of the chart on the dividing line of the first house – the house associated with the self, how you appear to others, and the lens through which you view the world. The Rising sign is the position from where the other houses and zodiac signs are drawn in a counter-clockwise direction.

CHART RULER: The planetary ruler of a person's Rising zodiac sign is always a key player in unlocking a birth chart and obtaining a deeper understanding of it.

A SIMPLE BIRTH CHART INTERPRETATION FOR A PISCES SUN PERSON

BIRTH CHART FOR CARA BORN 10 MARCH 1989 IN SHREWSBURY.

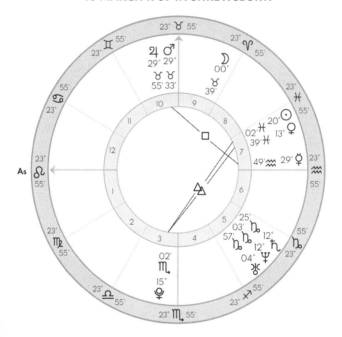

THE POSITION OF THE PLANETS: Cara has Leo rising. The Sun is in Pisces, the Moon is in Taurus, Mercury is in Aquarius, Venus sits in Pisces, Mars and Jupiter are in Taurus, Saturn, Neptune and Uranus are all in Capricorn and Pluto is sitting in Scorpio.

INTERPRETATION BASICS

As well as the signs the planets are in, also note their house positions. How do you begin to put all these signs and symbols together? It's usually best to begin with the Sun, Rising sign (As) and then to examine the condition of the Moon sign.

SUN, MOON, RISING SIGN (AS) AND CHART RULER: Cara's Sun is in gentle, emotional Pisces in the seventh house of relationships, so she'll likely be a particularly diplomatic, sociable (seventh) easy-going person who places her loved ones at the centre of her life (Sun). Her Rising sign (As) falls in self-confident, sunny Leo, which should lend her introverted Pisces Sun character a little more drama and authority. Leo Rising people deal with life's changes (Rising/As) in an ebullient, optimistic way, and expect to be liked and admired. As the Sun is the ruler of Leo, her chart ruler also becomes the Sun, lending further weight to her creative talents and willpower. Cara's Moon shines from the ninth house (travel/ philosophy) and is in strong, determined Taurus. This is an auspicious place for the Moon as it shakes up Taurus's dislike of change and makes for a more adventurous person. Taurus Moon people are usually emotionally stable, good with money and even-tempered, and the ninth house influence should make Cara very curious about other cultures and philosophies.

OTHER PLANETS: Cara's Mercury (communication) is in obsessively curious Aquarius in the seventh house of other people and relationships. Cara finds other people quite fascinating and with her other seventh house placement would do well as a relationship counsellor, psychologist or any job where she would need to study human behaviour. She's probably something of a genius (Aquarius) in solving other people's problems (seventh house).

Continuing with the relationship theme, Cara's Venus (love/talents) is in romantic Pisces, also in the seventh house of other people, and is conjunct (strengthening) the Sun. Cara will likely have considerable Pisces skills. She could be a gifted musician, dancer or artist, or just be blessed with a wonderful imagination. In a romantic relationship she may be drawn to ethereal, emotional (Pisces) people, or lost soul types who need an anchor in life to give them direction.

Cara's Mars (action) and Jupiter (fortune/optimism) are conjunct (strengthening) in Taurus in her tenth house of career and ambitions. This is a powerful combination that points to a firm career plan and, with Taurus in the tenth, could indicate a profession in banking, house building, farming, or the food industry. Jupiter there too expands all that it touches, adding a hefty dose of luck and cheerfulness into the bargain.

Saturn, Neptune and Uranus were all in the sign of Capricorn when Cara was born, and in the fifth house of creativity, children and drama. This is a stellium formation, when three or more planets act like a mega conjunction, strengthening the area of the chart in which they are found. Cara's imagination (Neptune), need for change (Uranus) and sense of authority

(Saturn), are all focused on the creative, fun and joyful side of life. Cara is probably naturally gifted at making things happen and, as ambitious Capricorn is the focus, she'll never give up until she has climbed to the top! Cara's Pluto (power/resources) sits in its own sign of Scorpio, a generational influence that shows great willpower and an ability to transform the planet. As it's in Cara's third house of communication we can guess that when she speaks or writes, others listen.

ADDING IN THE PLANETARY ASPECTS

Let's take a brief look at the strongest aspects – the ones with the most exact angles or 'orbs' to the planetary degrees (the numbers next to the planets).

SUN TRINE PLUTO: Cara has a confident and powerfully strong (Pluto) ego (Sun) which helps her get to the bottom of any challenges and generally works in her favour (trine).

MERCURY SQUARE MARS AND JUPITER: Mentally (Mercury), Cara experiences challenges (square) as she can be a little too exuberant and optimistic (Jupiter) in her thinking, leading her to make hasty (Mars) decisions.

VENUS TRINE PLUTO: Cara's relationships and talents (Venus) have the power to positively (trine) transform (Pluto) her life.

MARS CONJUNCT JUPITER: When Cara decides to take action or control (Mars), she attracts luck and good fortune (Jupiter) that she can then use to better her circumstances and the outcome.

SATURN CONJUNCT NEPTUNE: Cara can use her imagination (Neptune) in a powerful way (conjunction) to open doors in her job or career (Saturn).

YOUR JOB AS AN ASTROLOGER

The interpretation above is simplified to help you understand some of the nuts and bolts of interpretation. There are almost as many techniques and tools for analysing birth charts as there are people. Remember when you're putting the whole thing together that astrology doesn't show negatives or positives. The planets represent potential and opportunities, rather than definitions set in stone. It's your job as an astrologer to use the planets' wisdom to blend and synthesise those energies to create the picture of a whole person.

Going deeper

To see your own birth chart visit: www.astro.com and click the Free Horoscopes link and then enter your birth information. If you don't know what time you were born, put in 12.00pm. Your Rising sign and the houses might not be right, but the planets will be in the correct zodiac signs and the aspects will be accurate.

Further reading and credits

WWW.ASTRO.COM

This amazing astrological resource is extremely popular with both experienced and beginner astrologers. It's free to sign up and obtain your birth chart and personalised daily horoscopes.

BOOKS

PARKER'S ASTROLOGY by Derek and Julia Parker (Dorling Kindersley)

THE LITTLE BOOK OF ASTROLOGY by Marion Williamson (Summersdale)

THE BIRTHDAY ORACLE by Pam Carruthers (Arcturus)

THE 12 HOUSES by Howard Sasportas (London School of Astrology)

THE ARKANA DICTIONARY OF ASTROLOGY by Fred Gettings (Penguin)

THE ROUND ART by AJ Mann (Paper Tiger)

THE LUMINARIES by Liz Greene (Weiser)

SUN SIGNS by Linda Goodman (Pan Macmillan)

Marion Williamson is a best-selling astrology author and editor. *The Little Book of Astrology* and *The Little Book of the Zodiac* (Summersdale 2018) consistently feature in Amazon's top 20 astrology books. These were written to encourage beginners to move past Sun signs and delve into what can be a lifetime's study. Marion has been writing about different areas of self-discovery for over 30 years. A former editor of *Prediction* magazine for ten years, Marion had astrology columns in *TVTimes*, *TVEasy*, *Practical Parenting*, *Essentials* and *Anglers Mail* for over ten years. Twitter: @_I_am_astrology

Pam Carruthers is a qualified professional Vedic and Western astrologer and student of *A Course in Miracles*. An experienced Life Coach and Trainer, Pam helps clients discover the hidden patterns that are holding them back in their lives. A consultation with her is a life enhancing and healing experience. She facilitates a unique transformational workshop 'Healing your Birth Story' based on your birthchart. Based in the UK, Pam has an international clientele.

All images courtesy of Shutterstock and Freepik/Flaticon.com.